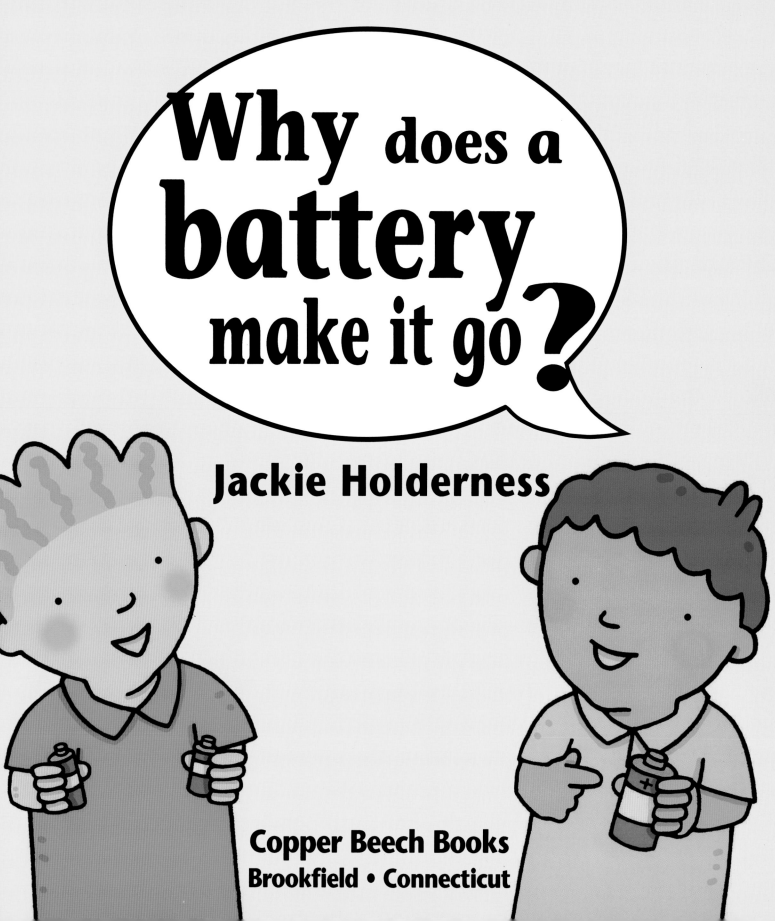

Why does a battery make it go?

Jackie Holderness

Copper Beech Books
Brookfield • Connecticut

Why does a battery make it go?

Today is Zack's birthday. His friends have come to his party. The children are having fun. Amy, Jo, and Steve are dancing to the CD player.

2

Why it works

When you plug an appliance into a wall socket and turn it on, electricity from the socket gives it energy to move or make light, sound, or heat. This electricity comes into your home from a power station. Chemicals inside a battery also make electricity. But you must match up the plus signs (+) and the minus signs (-) on the battery with the signs inside the machine so the electricity can flow.

Solve the puzzle!

What appliances use electricity in your house? Write down a list, or make a chart like the one on page 22.

We need to match the + and - signs on the batteries with the + and - signs on the machine.

3

It works! Batteries provide electricity like the electricity in your house. But they must be put in the right way.

4

Why does electricity work?

Now it's time for Zack to open his presents. Amy gives him a lamp and Zack's mom plugs it into the wall. Steve gives Zack a toy robot. Zack is putting batteries into its back to make it work.

Lots of my presents use electricity. But how does electricity work?

7

SAFETY FIRST!

NEVER touch a light bulb that has just been turned off! Always make sure it has cooled down first!

Let's see how the children find out.

3

Let's try a second bulb. I'll connect it here so it still makes a loop.

That works, too! So the wires must make a loop for the electricity to flow.

Why it works

Electricity only flows in a loop. Here the battery, wires, and bulb make a loop, or circuit. The battery makes electricity flow along the wire to the bulb, then back to the battery along the other wire. Two or more bulbs can be connected to one battery, but the wires must always make a circuit. In a house, the lights are connected by one or more circuits.

Solve the puzzle

What happens when you try lighting two bulbs? Make a circuit using two bulbs. Are they as bright as one bulb on its own? 9

What do switches do?

It's time for Zack's birthday cake. He takes a big breath to blow out all the candles with one big puff! Everyone is ready to sing "Happy Birthday."

Mom, can you turn off the lights, please?

10

How does the switch turn out the lights over here? A wire must connect them.
I think the switch blocks the electricity.
Maybe the switch breaks the loop so the electricity can't move around.
What do you think?

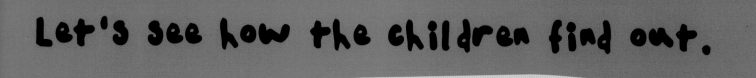

1

Let's use our circuit with the bulb and the battery.

If I unclip one of the wires, the bulb goes off. But how does a switch turn it on and off?

Zack's dad made this switch. Two thumbtacks are stuck into a block of wood.

2

The paper clip moves so it touches both of them or leaves a space.

12

Let's add the switch to the circuit. When the paper clip touches both thumbtacks, the bulb glows.

3

But if I swing the paper clip away, we make a break in the circuit and the bulb goes out.

4

Why it works

When Jo moves the paper clip, she makes a break in the circuit and the bulb goes out. If there is a break in any circuit, the electricity cannot flow around in a loop, so it does not flow at all. Most switches have a piece of metal that moves like the paper clip, so the circuit can be broken or connected.

Solve the puzzle

Which metals make good switches? Try using coins, a fork, a gold or silver ring, or a strip of aluminum foil. Use a simple circuit with a bulb and battery.

13

Why are wires covered with plastic?

The next day, the children go to play in Steve's yard. Steve's dad has been mowing the lawn with an electric mower. Now he is winding up its long cord, which had been plugged into a socket inside the house.

Why do electric wires and cords have plastic on the outside?

I think plastic keeps them dry. Mom said it's dangerous to touch anything electric with wet hands.
Then don't squirt water at me! Maybe plastic helps electricity flow along the wire.
I think the plastic keeps the electricity from getting out.
What do you think?

Let's see how the children find out.

Let's see if electricity flows through plastic, string, wool, metal, or china.

We can test them with our bulb and battery circuit.

1

If you clip the two wires to the ends of the plastic straw, the bulb doesn't come on.

The wool, china plate, and string didn't work either.

2

16

3

I'll try this metal spoon. Now the bulb is glowing again!

So electricity flows along the metal parts of a cord, but the plastic keeps it from flowing anywhere else.

Why it works

Electricity flows easily along some materials. We call them conductors. Many metals are very good conductors, so they are used in electric wires. Other materials, like plastic, stop the flow of electricity. They are called insulators. Plastic is used to cover metal wires so electricity can't flow out and harm you.

Solve the puzzle

Why do you think it's very dangerous to touch anything electric with wet hands? Think about whether electricity can flow through water.

17

How can electricity make a magnet?

The children are playing inside. Amy is doing some experiments with a set of magnets and the boys are playing with Steve's toy crane.

So many appliances use electricity. It makes a lamp light up, a fan spin, and a CD player play music.

Electric batteries also make this crane pick up these paper clips.

19

Let's see how the children find out.

We need a piece of wire about twice as long as I am. Mom said we should wrap it around this long steel nail.

1

I've left some wire loose at both ends, so we can connect them to the battery.

2

Let's see if it works like a magnet. We can test it with these metal paper clips.

Why it works

A wire works like a magnet when electricity flows through it. Its magnetic strength can be increased by wrapping it around an iron nail. When you turn off the electricity, the magnet stops working. The magnetic effect of electricity can also be used to make motors turn in washing machines, fans, and CD players.

Solve the puzzle

How can you test the power of a battery? Make a magnet like Steve's and connect it to different types of battery. See which one picks up the most paper clips.

21

Did you solve the puzzles?

What appliances use electricity in your house?

You can probably find lots of things that use electricity in your house. But be careful what you touch! Make a chart showing appliances that use electricity from a socket and things that use batteries.

Electricity from socket	Electricity from battery
Lamp	Flashlight
Refrigerator	Watch
Stove	Camera
Hairdryer	Car lights
Television	Cell phone
CD player	CD player

What happens when you try lighting two bulbs?

Two light bulbs in a simple circuit with one battery (above) don't shine as brightly as one bulb on its own. But see how bright they are if you arrange the bulbs and battery in a circuit like the one below.

Which metals make good conductors?

Most do. Electricity flows easily through metals such as iron, brass, copper, silver, and aluminum, so they are good conductors. Copper is often used to make electrical wires.

How can you test the power of a battery?

The battery that makes the magnet pick up the most paper clips is giving the magnet the most power. If you add an extra battery to the circuit, does the magnet pick up even more paper clips?

Why is it dangerous to touch anything electric with wet hands?

Electricity flows easily through water, so if your hands get wet (like Amy on page 15), be careful not to touch any electric plugs or appliances. The electricity flowing through them could give you a serious electrical shock.

Index

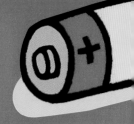

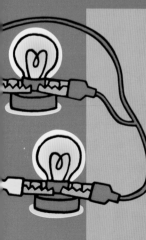

© Aladdin Books Ltd 2002

10 9 8 7 6 5 4 3 2 1

Designed and produced by
Aladdin Books Ltd
28 Percy Street
London W1T 2BZ

First published in
the United States in 2002 by
Copper Beech Books,
an imprint of
The Millbrook Press
2 Old New Milford Road
Brookfield, Connecticut 06804

ISBN 0-7613-2820-3 (Library bdg.)
ISBN 0-7613-1738-4 (Trade h'cover)
ISBN 0-7613-1841-0 (Paper ed.)

Cataloging-in-Publication data is
on file at the Library of Congress.

Printed in U.A.E.
All rights reserved

Editor
Jim Pipe

Science Consultants
Helen Wilson and David Coates
Westminster Institute of Education
Oxford Brookes University

Science Tester
Alex Laar

Design
Flick, Book Design and Graphics

Illustration
Jo Moore